Stay Inspir

2-

3

Stay Inspired

Finding Motivation for Your Creative Work

Brandon Stosuy

Abrams Image,
New York

Editor: Hayley Salmon
Freelance Editor: Karrie Witkin
Designers: Kristian Henson
and Jenice Kim
Production Manager: Larry
Pekarek

Library of Congress Control
Number: 2020944921

ISBN: 978-1-4197-4652-9
eISBN: 978-1-64700-377-7

Text © 2021
Brandon Stosuy

Cover © 2021 Abrams

Printed and bound in China
10 9 8 7 6 5 4 3 2 1

Abrams Image books are
available at special discounts
when purchased in quantity
for premiums and promotions
as well as fundraising or educational use. Special editions
can also be created to spec-
ification. For details, contact
specialsales@abramsbooks.
com or the address below.

Abrams Image® is a regis-
tered trademark of Harry N.
Abrams, Inc.

ABRAMS The Art of Books
195 Broadway, New York, NY 10007
abramsbooks.com

Contents

"There's a mythological artist that I sometimes wonder about—someone who goes in and knows exactly what the work is and follows the formula and has it all figured out. That mythological life seems easier. It's also antithetical to all of my interests— the creative process itself, play, discovery, and push/pull around the idea of 'too much.'"

Annie Bielski
(Visual artist, writer)

"A line gets framed somehow, and whether I'm watching a movie or outside or just woke up, I have to immediately write it down. Sometimes I can tell when I'm going to write a poem, like I'm in a state. But the only ritual for poetry is a kind of attentiveness, being aware of myself and not letting a line dissipate."

Eileen Myles
(Poet, writer, author of
Chelsea Girls, *Cool for You*)

There's a stereotypical notion of "inspiration." In that scenario you may see a flash of light or some kind of mystical visitation; you're struck by an idea and creativity flows from you, uncontrollably, as if you're possessed. This has never happened to me. Inspiration is more complex and complicated than that, and usually not quite so dramatic. Which isn't to say it's less magical: Finding an idea you want to keep and continue to grow is exciting.

The thunderbolt notion of inspiration, while poetically appealing, is a bit passive. The process of inspiration, which takes time and trial and error, is active. So let's begin by removing the idea of inspiration as something *happening to you* and reframe it as something you can *make happen*.

Real-life inspiration involves problem-solving, playing, researching, reworking, and engaging in a variety of ways. Consider it a kind of curiosity: Something piques your interest and you feel compelled to pursue it further, to understand it better. You try to be attentive to the everyday. You think about your past. You talk to friends. Sometimes, inspiration emerges via another person or many other people. When everything's working, it's a state of creative flow or imaginative play.

When talking with writer Maggie Nelson for my website, The Creative Independent, she said to me: "It's key to keep finding new things that inspire and not just melting into some broken record of how things went for you."* She's right.

Something I've learned from personal experience is that when you *do* find your central concerns—the things that inspire you—you return to them over and over. But try not to get mired in them: Inspiration provides the fuel for pushing forward and finding newer pockets and outlets for your interests and concerns. Use the things that speak to you as signposts to help you figure out where to go next in life. If you keep following them, you'll discover a larger world of like-minded people and creative possibilities beyond your imagination.

As a teenager, living in a small farming town in New Jersey, I felt isolated from any kind of creative outlet until I discovered punk. Even after finding it, I was removed from a scene. Then I spotted some graffiti on the side of a small building in my hometown: It was the mascot of the punk band the Misfits, and it became a sign and invocation to keep exploring punk and to find others who were into it, too. I started seeking out punk bands in the area and putting together shows in the field behind my house. I embarked on the kind of work that I continue to do in the present.

*Stosuy, Brandon, "Interview: Maggie Nelson," The Creative Independent, December 29, 2016.

Thirty years later, while working on this book, I lear[n]
Melissa Auf der Maur—one of my long-standing collabor[...]
had also been deeply inspired by the Misfits. Melissa and [...]
been producing a music and arts festival, Basilica Soundscape,
together since 2011. Melissa played bass for Hole and Smashing
Pumpkins, and at one point worked on a duet with Glenn Danzig,
the Misfits' lead singer. Somehow, I never knew about that.
Learning this helped explain our immediate connection back when
we first met. As kids, we'd been attracted to a similar mythology
and music, and I like to think that by following some of the same
signs, our paths brought us to working together.

I've spent the majority of my adult life in cities, but while
writing this book, I ended up relocating to a farm in rural Penn-
sylvania for a few months. Watching my kids, who've lived their
entire young lives in Brooklyn, get a version of my childhood
experience was inspiring. It reopened a lot of things I'd forgotten
about and had me digging deep into my knowledge base for
things I never had to teach them in Brooklyn: identifying poison
ivy, the proper way to pick blueberries, how to remove a tick,
why you shouldn't pick up a snapping turtle, and how to shoot
a BB gun. It's been eye-opening to see that the kind of environment I'd found stifling as a kid has been so enriching for them.

It's also been a reminder not to dismiss our own experiences,
as small or boring as they may seem, and to also slow down and
appreciate what you have on hand, right there around you. What
may seem obvious or quotidian to you is new and unfamiliar to
someone else.

Stay Inspired offers a series of strategies for unblocking mental barriers and finding new ways to approach your creative work. When I'm inspired, I feel a genuine connection to something. I want to explore it more. It's an instinctively generative feeling. I think of being inspired as a sense of momentum, of moving forward and building on experiences, and forging my own path in life. It goes beyond making art.

What is your own relationship to inspiration right now? Maybe you have too many ideas and are having trouble following through on any of them. Maybe you haven't experienced a state of creative flow in a while and worry that you're running out of ideas. Are you bored? Unchallenged? Or is this a particularly challenging time? If you've been disrupted or need to make a change, being inspired is the perfect state of mind for problem-solving and figuring out where to go next.

Before we go further, let's begin with a few questions to define your entry point in this process:

Do you want to generate new ideas or are you juggling too many? Are you unsure about how to begin a creative project or where to take it next?

Both

unsure how to start or if I have

enough to start

tired

lazy

Describe how you feel when you are genuinely engaged and inspired (or the last time you felt that way). What is the situation and what are you doing?

happy & full of light, intelligent, connected
Eastridge Interiors

Why is it important to you to stay inspired?

it's how I feel alive; connected to life

1

Background and Beginnings

Start with yourself, where you came from, and what grabs your attention

Idols and Influences

2

Turn to your heroes and mentors and make work in conversation with theirs

Collaboration and Community

4

Reach out, let go of ego, share your work, and share resources

Go deep, go wide, and find unlikely connections between your interests

Curiosity and Research

3

Stay Inspired is the second volume in a three-part series that is designed to demystify the creative process and guide people through different aspects of a creative life. I divided this book into four chapters, each one representing a different path for coming up with ideas and building on them: Background and Beginnings, Idols and Influences, Curiosity and Research, and Community and Collaboration.

In each section, I offer my own stories, while weaving in advice, revelations, and experiences of different types of working artists, including musicians, authors, filmmakers, dancers, designers, and visual artists. There are a number of different voices here, suggesting a wide variety of approaches to getting inspired. As I did with the first book in the series, *Make Time for Creativity*, I approached friends and people I've collaborated with at one time or another with the aim of making the book feel like a community gathering.

Their thoughts led me to create prompts to help you meditate, and act upon, staying inspired. That's a huge part of this: Nobody's approach will be exactly the same as yours, and it shouldn't be. What's important to keep in mind as you read *Stay Inspired*, is that you are finding ways to unlock your own creative flow. For most artists that I know, this is an ongoing and cyclical process.

There won't be lightning bolts, but I hope you experience more than a few flashes of insight.

Let's begin.

"I want to stay excited in my writing and artmaking, and I always want to be a beginner in some way. I must be curious to find out what I can and can't do. And I guess I must have some kind of deep confidence in my talent, or maybe, I mean, in the power of my interest to make something."

Dennis Cooper
(Writer, author of The George Miles Cycle, *The Sluts*, *My Loose Thread*)

In this chapter, we'll look closely at ourselves as a resource for creative inspiration. We'll look at our origins, the specifics of where we came from, and the things around us that first grabbed our attention.

We're beginning here, with our enthusiasms and limitations, and we'll use both to define a point of view that's 100 percent our own. You might feel some resistance to this kind of self-focus, and that's totally normal. Perhaps you're thinking there's nothing "special" about your background—definitely nothing inspiring. Maybe you've moved on, physically and emotionally, a long time ago.

I can relate. I'd always thought I "hated" my hometown, a small working-class part of rural New Jersey far away from any discernible creative activity. Living in isolation forced me to go inward—to entertain myself—and to go outward in search of more like-minded people. As a teenager, I began to create what I felt was missing from my environment, but to do this I had to use the few resources at hand.

That dichotomy of attempting to transcend the limitations of place while being firmly grounded by those limitations became the keystone of my creative philosophy and aesthetic. I used what was available to me, and what I had available to me was unique.

What you have available to you is unique, too.

Rooted in Place

I grew up in a farming town of eight hundred people, a place made of pine needles, sand, and space. I didn't have access to a local community, and until I could drive, I needed to be inventive with how I spent my time. I defined my situation as "boredom," but in retrospect it's why I spent so much time reading and learning. I wasn't particularly smart or disciplined as a kid, I just didn't have anything else to do.

Nobody immediately around me was into the things I found myself drawn to—one of my stepfathers used to call me "college boy" for wanting to read novels—so my first creative instinct was that I would have to find like-minded people outside of Chatsworth.

I was introduced to punk through a friend's older sister, who was home from college and let me borrow a few cassettes. A big part of punk culture is DIY. Discovering punk was my starting point for wanting to create my own work—not for school or a job—but because I wanted to do it. I sought out as many things related to punk as I could. I begged my mom to drive me into Philadelphia and then wait outside of record stores where I'd nervously purchase records and zines from older, cooler people with complicated hair and spiked accessories.

But the biggest creative catalyst for me ended up being something right near Chatsworth: a smiling, hooded skull spray-painted on the side of a cinder-block building at the edge of a local blueberry farm. If you didn't know what it meant, it was a random black-ink skeleton head, but if you did know where it came from, it was the spooky, charming logo for the New Jersey punk band the Misfits. It had likely been there for years—the band started in 1977, when I was four—though I didn't see it until I was a teenager.

You can pass something every day, but until it has resonance for you, it remains invisible. Punk is what decoded that graffiti for me. I was looking for some kind of pathway to somewhere else, and this felt like a lesson and a clue. There *was* someone else out there, and they weren't that far away. It added an exclamation point to the bent mailboxes, horseflies, and scrub pine that I associated with my long walks through the woods around my home.

Place leaves a mark—living where I did defined my creative process. I took the exposure to punk that I could get, tried to recreate it in my own world, and ended up producing things unique to a teenager in rural New Jersey in the early nineties. Those experiences informed a creative philosophy that I still use today.

You can't curate exactly where you grow up, but it plays an important part in curating you. If you look back on your childhood and teenage years without judgement, you may find the ingredients of your personal aesthetic or creative approach—one that has roots in daydreaming, play, and even boredom.

"The starting point for me has always been place."

Matthew Barney*

(Multimedia artist, creator of *The Cremaster Cycle*)

Matthew Barney has talked to me about how, growing up in Idaho, he was drawn to the area's natural beauty. He knew the story of Ernest Hemingway's suicide in Ketchum, Idaho, and saw it as part of the general landscape and mythology of the area. When he first moved to New York City as an adult, he'd look for traces of Idaho's mountains and ravines in the Manhattan skyline.

If you don't feel a strong connection to where you grew up—either because you moved around frequently or perhaps felt detached from the place—take a moment to think about the natural landscape and built environments of your childhood. What was considered beautiful, important, and safe? What was forgotten, marginal, dangerous, or off-limits? What do you associate with the words "center" and "frontier"?

Think about how your childhood environment defined your relationship to space. Did you spend a lot of time looking up, down, between things, through windows and frames, or into the distance? For example, someone who grew up in a wide, flat place would be drawn to look up into the immense sky, whereas someone living up high would train their eye to the world below. Your perception is formed through this process, and so is your imagination. Conscious of it or not, you take this perspective— a piece of wherever you are from—with you wherever you go.

*Stosuy, Brandon, "Matthew Barney on Idaho," The Creative Independent, October 6, 2016.

Point of View

Take a moment to ponder the questions on the previous page and jot down the associations and sense perceptions (sounds, scents) that you connect to the environments of your childhood.

_____

_____

_____

_____

_____

_____

_____

_____

_____

_____

_____

_____

_____

_____

_____

_____

_____

Your childhood home represents a world with its own culture and rules, where certain activities and beliefs are encouraged or discouraged. Your stance toward creativity was shaped in this environment. My friend, visual artist Matthew Day Jackson, grew up surrounded by people who "knew how to make stuff—from race cars to dolls," which means that collaboration and craft are central to his definition of creativity. Someone from a family in which each person does their own thing might think of creativity as a solitary pursuit. Consider these contrasting experiences:

"My parents were not the kind that made me feel cozy and loved at home, but the kind that had me chomping at the bit to get out in the world and dive deeply into all I loved. They both started in the worlds of journalism and activism; they had their own radio and TV shows, founded leftist magazines, and had amazing friends. They took me on life-changing trips before I turned twelve. We stayed on people's couches in Africa, England, France, Hungary, and Spain. That affected my worldview the most: There are people like us everywhere, and they have *fun*!"

Melissa Auf der Maur
(Musician, photographer, bassist of Hole and Smashing Pumpkins, cofounder of Basilica Soundscape)

"I think my family despised working jobs. Reading was the drug of choice, and everybody loved art, though my parents were clueless as to how you would get around to making it. The fact that they didn't want to be working stiffs and were in fact dreamers was a real provocation for me. They felt, and we felt, like we didn't fit 'here.' My mother loved to read aloud, which is essentially what I do for a living. So I learned a lot at home."

Eileen Myles
(Poet, writer, author of *Chelsea Girls*, *Cool for You*)

"I grew up with a single mother in a working-class suburb of Philadelphia. The focus was always more on getting through the day than the proverbial broadening of horizons. People in my neighborhood were into sports and not much else. I always felt out of place. I don't think it's a coincidence that so much of what I consider to be good metal, punk, and hardcore is born out of the working class. For me, it's art that exists as a reaction to the fear and alienation that comes with poverty and being perpetually misunderstood."

Michael Berdan
(Musician, writer, vocalist of Uniform)

Cultural Habitat

Reflecting on the experiences shared on the previous pages, think about how creativity (or cultivating a sense of wonder, freedom to explore, and avenues to express yourself) was modeled and encouraged (or perhaps absent) in your childhood home.

_____

_____

_____

_____

_____

_____

_____

_____

_____

_____

_____

_____

_____

_____

_____

_____

Your childhood experiences are rich terrain for discovering personal metaphors. Each of us comes from a specific landscape and point of view, but we still need to excavate down to a subterranean, emotional level to find what is really ours. Take these two passages from Matt Berninger of The National, and Meg Duffy (aka Hand Habits), who both have childhood memories of following train tracks. The tracks take Matt back to a place of adventure, exertion, and freedom. For Meg, it's the opposite; the tracks are a reminder of being stuck.

"I spent a lot of my childhood on my Uncle Jack's Christmas tree farm in Lawrenceburg, Indiana. I'm only now starting to notice how many of my favorite images come from experiences on that farm. My cousins and I would spend days camping, walking the railroad tracks, and hiking the creeks and woods. My older cousins would sometimes jump onto moving freight trains and we'd have to catch up with them an hour later down the tracks. Everything felt wild and free and dangerous. There's some of that in the song 'Walk It Back': 'I walk through Lawrencetown, along the tracks. My own body in my arms but I won't collapse.'"

Matt Berninger
(Musician, writer, vocalist of The National)

"As I get older, I find little clues that lead me back to where I grew up. I often am not consciously thinking of those artifacts from a place I harbored a lot of resentment toward—for its lack—but lately I've been trying to be back there mentally and emotionally and find myself walking near the train tracks or by the boat launch. The train tracks, for me, always made me feel the working-class nature of the town I lived in. Rusty, loud, continuing through the night, carrying freight typically, but occasionally an Amtrak passenger train would roll by. I always thought I'd never be able to leave, that traveling would be something intangible, speeding by and reserved for other people. The train still runs through the town . . . and I think of it as the ghost that remains, a way to always get back to the feeling."

Meg Duffy
(Singer-songwriter, guitarist,
performs as Hand Habits)

Abecedarium

Use each letter of the alphabet to catalog twenty-six objects that you associate with memories from your childhood. These don't need to be huge events; in fact, small moments and ultra-specific associations are better. For example, maybe "P" is Parking Lot, where you had your first date in front of a 7-Eleven.

A _____

B _____

C _____

D _____

E _____

F _____

G _____

H _____

I _____

J _____

K _____

L

M

N

O

P

Q

R

S

T

U

V

W

X

Y

Z

What forms of play engaged you as a kid? Through games and pretending, we create scenarios and structures to explore possibility, novelty, and uncertainty. Typically, we're stressed by uncertainty, but when we're "just playing" we're in control and find enjoyment in the unknown. Musician Meg Duffy and writer Dennis Cooper succinctly describe how childhood play relates to their creative processes, and how it trained both of them to build worlds and summon emotional responses through their art.

"I can remember as a young child being really invested in playing pretend. Pretending to be someone else (usually a boy, often named Jason) with my cousins and running around and climbing trees as these different people. I think this archetype of fantasy was my first glimpse into exaggerating the real, which is something I feel I do as a songwriter. I would pretend to be tough, or invisible, or I would pretend to die. Now when I'm writing lyrics, any emotion can be zoomed in on and made real in the song."

Meg Duffy
(Singer-songwriter, guitarist,
performs as Hand Habits)

"The earliest things I remember being hugely influenced by and excited about were amusement parks. I'm sure my writing was influenced by the way they were organized physically, the intricacy of the rides, the closed-off worlds they created, the way they used the charismatic aspects of the colorful and charming as lures, and how they sought to control the experiences of being afraid or happy. I was always super-creative as a kid before I found writing. I made walk-through haunted house attractions in my basement every Halloween, and I built funfairs in my backyard every summer with booths and rides and things and advertised them in the neighborhood, and I turned our attic into a theater and put on plays, all when I was nine, ten, and eleven years old."

Dennis Cooper

(Writer, author of The George Miles Cycle, *The Sluts, My Loose Thread*)

Toying with Emotions

Look at the list of objects and associated experiences in your abecedarium on page 30. Do any speak to you as a kind of creative evocation or prompt: an image for a poem, the title of a short story, a prompt for a photograph or painting? Choose one object and explore the emotions that you associate with it. How might these be exaggerated or amplified in your piece? Jot down ideas here.

_____

_____

_____

_____

_____

_____

_____

_____

_____

_____

_____

_____

_____

_____

"The imaginary world you occupy as a kid, in playing make-believe or reading stories . . . I don't feel like it's too far off from what I do now, when I'm writing. There's something very innocent about any creative pursuit. I'm more inspired as a writer not when I'm disciplinary toward myself, but when I'm more permissive and forgiving and flexible and open. It's a good reminder, since I often forget."

Ling Ma
(Writer, critic, teacher, author of *Severance*)

Message Meets Medium

The most important outlet I had for creativity as a teenager was my zine. Initially I called it *Nasal Spray*, after my dad's use of nasal spray to combat his allergies, and later *White Bread*, as an acknowledgement of my "white trash" town and the flavorless bread most people purchased and I restocked at Cumberland Farms where I started working at fifteen.

The late eighties and early nineties were a heyday for small punk zines. I discovered the Bay Area punk zine *Maximum Rocknroll* at a record store I visited in Philadelphia, which then led me to MRR's *Book Your Own Fuckin' Life*, a DIY resource that became a bible for me. I also found *Cometbus*, a romantic, rambling diaristic zine by a guy named Aaron Cometbus.

So with some knowledge of the form, I started my own. It's funny, I had read a bunch, but I wasn't sure how the word "zine" was pronounced. I thought it rhymed with "pine," because I'd never heard anyone actually speak the word. I wasn't an expert, but I loved reading, I loved books, and this felt like a way to enter that world in a low-risk and low-cost way. I could sit at my desk in a musty basement with my typewriter, glue stick, and scissors, and that was all I needed to bring one of these to life.

White Bread taught me how to write. It's how I found my voice. I wrote about everything that came to mind: my worries, fears, embarrassments, hopes, and insecurities. I reviewed my lunches over the course of a week. I analyzed an unrequited crush. I talked about the time I thought maybe I wanted to die. Nothing was off-limits. I'd take notes for the zine when I worked at my various part-time jobs. I'd then go home and write and not worry about editing. I just let it pour out.

I wrote about my life, at first, because I had nobody to talk to. After a while, I'd bring copies to school and share them with friends. Then I graduated to sending issues of *White Bread* to *Factsheet Five*, a newsprint publication that reviewed zines, and my readership broadened a little bit. Eventually, I learned that you could submit zines to Tower Records, and they'd place an order for distribution if they thought it was sellable. I did that, and the first time in, Tower took 350 copies. This led to a small feature in the glossy publication *Alternative Press*, which then led to more distro.

It was exciting at first just to send the zines out into the world. Over time, the distributors would get back to me and ask for more copies. I started receiving long letters, mixtapes, and other homemade zines from people I'd never met. The process was step-by-step and organic, but a project that had started out of loneliness led me to a community and an audience.

I didn't think of it at the time as a learning experience, but making a zine taught me about organization, multitasking, customer care, and finishing what you started. I had control over all aspects of it and could do it all on my own, which was thrilling. When you're a teenager, you don't have control over much, but I had control over this.

"The ability to record and listen back was deeply important to us right from the start. Even using a simple boom box and cassette tape in the 1990s gave us a way to zoom out. As young writers, our voices were a mystery, as were our minds, and that allowed us to break rules and follow our gut in a way that was exhilarating. There were an infinite number of songs to write, and even with a guitar of broken strings, they were totally within reach. The lack of strings on the guitar forced us to be more creative with our voices. Experimenting with melodies, harmonies, and rhythms, our vocal cords became the instrument we wanted to master."

Sara Quin
(Musician, writer,
member of Tegan and Sara)

Simple Tools

Consider how a boom box and a guitar with three strings were beneficial to Sara Quin's songwriting with her twin sister, Tegan, in the earliest days of what would become Tegan and Sara. Limitations offer focus and a form. They force you to problem-solve. Look at your project ideas on page 34, or think about something that you've been wanting to make. How might you execute a version of it with the materials and time available to you? Give it a try and report back on the results.

Being a Beginner

Inspiration can be a form of problem-solving that kicks in when your skills and knowledge don't match what you want to achieve. You were in this position as a child almost constantly. When I started curating, for instance, I didn't know the word "curate," and had no real model for it. I just had the impulse to put things together. Because I was creating alone, without the pressure of the Internet or even a local community where folks instantly weighed in on what I'd made, I realized it was OK to fail. What was important was to avoid getting caught up in the failure, to embrace a process of trial and error, and to keep pushing through to the next project.

Get reacquainted with the feeling of being a beginner by trying something totally new, low-stakes, and well outside of your expertise. List some options that you can explore.

_____

_____

_____

_____

_____

_____

_____

_____

_____

"As creative people, we all have our preferred methods, what we're 'known for,' but that can create unnecessary pressures about living up to our archives, about delivering a 'product.' Sometimes to jump into that creative space, we have to set ourselves up to comfortably stray from what we typically explore, or our typical methodology, and to try something different for a while with an open-ended sense of joy and playfulness."

Lavender Suarez
(Musician, sound healer,
performs as C. Lavender)

Cultivated Confidence

How we're encouraged when we're young—and the resources available to us—are encoded in our sense of self and where our "talent" lies. Consider these observations from Matt Berninger and Matthew Barney, who found entry points to their current practice through the disciplines that they focused on as kids and teenagers. Think about the skills that you've developed in one area as a reservoir of knowledge and confidence that you can draw on for new projects and totally different pursuits.

"I took piano for a couple of years but was turned off by a traumatic recital where I must have had a minor panic attack. I never took music lessons of any kind after that. My parents sent me to an art class taught by a local mom, Mrs. Shute. It was the first time I remember having a sense that I was good at something. By the time I got to high school, I thought of myself as an artist. I always wanted to write songs and be in a band, but I had to get to it through visual art. I might use what I learned from visual art and design to write songs as much as anything I learned from music."

Matt Berninger
(Musician, writer,
vocalist of The National)

"I realized . . . that the most legible experiences I could draw upon as an artist were the athletic ones from my childhood and teenage years. One of the things that interested me the most in athletics was the way the body develops and [that] performance is improved and enhanced under resistance. So, just as I was feeling compelled to put my body into my work, and into the performed actions, I had to accept that my relationship to my own body and to bodies in general, was formed in an athletic environment. This is the model of making I understood the best, so it carried over into the studio."

Matthew Barney
(Multimedia artist, creator of
The Cremaster Cycle)

"As an only child, I spent a lot of time entertaining myself. One of the ways I did that was reading. Another was staring into space for hours at a time: on the couch, in my room, in the backyard, in our neighbor's tree."

Sarah Gerard
(Writer, author of *Binary Star*, *Sunshine State*, *True Love*)

Did you have unstructured time as a kid, where you had literally nothing to do but stare into space? Maybe you were bored or maybe you were daydreaming. Your brain was making connections and exploring possibilities, but from a place of passivity. Nothing forced. It's important to check back into that state periodically, to allow your mind to do its own backroom work. It helps to think about the spaces that you once gravitated toward when you were alone with your thoughts: a tree, a dark hideout, an open field, a swing . . . Try to map that kind of place onto your present circumstance— or perhaps recreate it for yourself. Sketch it or make notes here.

Conclusion

The zines that I began making when I was thirteen gave me a medium for shaping my voice, and I found a community through them. But I reached a point where I wanted to create things in an actual, physical space. So I started doing punk shows; local bands would play and friends would attend. People sipped bottled seltzer and slam danced in the field behind my house.

When I was seventeen, once I got the hang of those kinds of events, I decided to go bigger. I just expanded my approach from the earlier shows I'd done, until I had a lineup of twenty-four bands spread across forty-eight hours. I didn't have a stage so we used the flatbed of a hay truck. I called the festival The Indie 500, a play on the term "indie rock" and the big car race. Over the course of the weekend, a few hundred people passed through. Through ticket sales ($5 per day, $7 for the weekend), merch (homemade T-shirts), and concessions (a sno-kone machine), we managed to clear $2,000, which felt like a fortune.

I made plenty of mistakes: I didn't know how to create a budget, I booked too many bands, I didn't think underage people would sneak in booze, I'd never considered the possibility that some-one would bring fireworks, and I didn't read the noise ordinances closely enough. I assumed that one porta potty would be enough.

But, stress aside, it was a success—and it gave me the con-fidence to keep going. I thought, *If I could pull this off with no budget and no materials, imagine what I could do with more?* It taught me to look at the details, not to assume someone would solve something for me, and to avoid boring everyday formats and the otherwise obvious.

Today I consciously avoid making events feel overly polished or needlessly formal. I also like aesthetic echoes. At Basilica Soundscape (the annual festival I cofounded with my friend Melissa) we have staged poetry readings in a trolley car; a little nod, for me, to the spirit of the Indie 500's hay-truck stage. When I worked for the music website Pitchfork, we used art museum basements and sculpture gardens for events instead of standard venues. It's what led me to places like parking garages (where Björk and I did a sweaty Cinco de Mayo DJ set), riverside docks, and factories.

Everything you do, from when you're a kid to now, is connected. Making this book—by writing personal essays and collecting thoughts from those I work with and admire—is directly connected to the zines I made as a teenager. If you're looking for a source of inspiration that is entirely yours, go back to your childhood:

> Think about how the landscape, the built environment, and the organization of your hometown shaped your perception as a child. Try amplifying that point of view in your work.
> Pinpoint specific memories that still resonate with you emotionally. Use this content as a jumping-off point and exaggerate the emotions. Test out whether something small and precious can stand in for the broad and universal.
> Recall the exact conditions of your childhood states of play, wonder, daydreaming, and boredom. Recreate those conditions for yourself now, giving your brain the opportunity to go about its own way of processing information and making connections.
> Be a beginner. Try something completely new, embrace limitations, and see what happens as a result of your problem-solving.

"Everything is derivative. Everything has been done in some form, some way before. Once you accept that then you're free. You can stop looking over your shoulder or furiously combing the Internet to make sure your exact iteration is unequivocally unique."

Carly Ayres
(Creative director, writer,
founder of 100sUnder100)

In this chapter, you'll identify your influences and idols and explore what inspires you about their work. We'll touch on the anxiety of influence and explore some strategies that enable you to enter into a conversation with your idols (rather than mimicking what you love).

One of my longest-standing influences is Ian MacKaye, a punk musician (Minor Threat, Fugazi) and the cofounder of the record label Dischord. Early on, I was drawn to his anthemic, angry music. Later, it was his business model that inspired me: He kept prices low, handled his own distribution, and showed me that you could do things on your own in a sustainable, professional way.

Over the years, I got to know Ian after interviewing him for Pitchfork. When I launched The Creative Independent, I had a conversation with him in front of an audience to inaugurate the site. The format of TCI was inspired by the utility of punk zines, so having Ian at this event felt important. He was one of the first heroes I discovered as a kid, and here he was, legitimately enthusiastic about a project that I'd completed as an adult.

Seeking out mentors—those who can directly influence your work and your life—is an important component of this chapter. At various points in my life, I've reached out to people I admire. I've included some stories of what happened as a result, and hope they inspire you to take similar chances.

As mentioned, my earliest influence was punk rock, and the larger community around it. My other influences were often kids my own age, making zines a lot like my zines, just a few towns and states over. As I got older and read more widely, I started to identify different writers who inspired me—individuals who felt like self-contained libraries. I was still figuring out the world, and they had the ability to create entire worlds with their words.

I discovered the ambitious, anarchic postmodern writer Thomas Pynchon while I was in high school. Pynchon discussed counterculture, politics, and music in his books. His work was serious, but slapstick. I was drawn to the idea that he lived largely in seclusion, that he didn't do press or readings. He literally let the work speak for itself.

Another, maybe even more unlikely influence for a teen with blue hair, was the author William H. Gass. I was seventeen when I first read his essays. I loved the way he blended the personal with the critical, and that he wasn't afraid to show vulnerability and humanity. His nonfiction felt linked to the personal writing of zines, but in service of explaining Samuel Beckett, Symbolist poetry, and Kafka. He also often gave advice to younger writers.

Because Gass seemed approachable in his essays, I wrote him a letter, and surprisingly, he wrote back. In my letter I told him I was trying to be a writer but wasn't sure it was working. I told him I was drawn to his notion that the best way to learn to write was to read, and I asked him for some recommendations. In his response, he suggested a number of authors and specific books (among them, Rilke's *The Notebooks of Malte Laurids Brigge*,

Thomas Mann's *The Magic Mountain*, Virginia Woolf's *Diaries*, and Gertrude Stein's *Three Lives*). His brief note, maybe ten lines, became a curriculum that guided me for the next couple of years and influenced all of my work.

I never actually wanted to write *like* Pynchon or Gass. It was their attitudes that interested me, despite their differences. Pynchon had only been photographed in public once and didn't show up to receive the awards he won. Gass taught university classes and would respond kindly to a letter from some random kid. But they both illustrated, for me, a completely personal approach to what they did. They carved out weird paths based on what they loved.

Gass's kindness inspired me to write to people I admired in the future, and it showed me community could exist outside of my comfort zone. It's why, after consuming four of his short, perfect novels in one weekend, I wrote to Dennis Cooper. He also wrote back. I ended up doing my graduate thesis on him, and we became good friends and collaborators. It also inspired how I react when people write to me. Gass's short letter, something I doubt he remembered sending, taught me the importance of helping others with advice when you have it.

It can feel daunting to put yourself out there, for sure, but it's worthwhile remembering that we're all human, and if you give it a shot, it's often worth it.

"I'm quite influenced by video games, which ties in with my early fascination with theme parks, and I learned a lot about narrative and spatial concerns and rhythm and stuff from playing them. Visual art is a big influence for much the same reason. Discovering John Baldessari's work as a teen was probably as important to my writing as finding Rimbaud or Marquis de Sade were, and sculptors like Charles Ray also fed me a lot of ideas regarding thinking about writing in a three-dimensional way."

Dennis Cooper
(Writer, author of The George Miles Cycle,
The Sluts, My Loose Thread)

Your Influences

What did you read, listen to, and watch when you were a kid?

_____

_____

_____

_____

_____

What did you read, listen to, and watch as a teenager/young adult?

_____

_____

_____

_____

_____

If someone approached you for a list of five things you find inspiring _at this very moment_, what would you put down?

_____

_____

_____

_____

_____

Look at your list of influences above. Are there any that seem at odds with each other? Does this indicate something about the development of your own taste/aesthetic?

"Fan letters are a way to tap into an actual conversation, explain how someone's work has affected you, and have a dialogue. Treating people like saviors or untouchable doesn't help anyone; it's necessary for there to be a back and forth."

Darcie Wilder
(Writer, author of *Literally Show Me a Healthy Person*)

"Fan letters are a good way to remind yourself what it is you care about. If you have to put your appreciation into two simple, non-wanky sentences, it can be clarifying and salutary. It sort of feels like setting your own compass."

Hermione Hoby
(Writer, critic, author of *Neon in Daylight*, *Virtue*)

Fan Mail

Write a letter to someone you admire. You could approach it
as Hermione Hoby suggests and express your appreciation of
something in just two sentences. Or you could ask for advice,
or maybe write about a project you're working on, or even
just talk a little about your day, to provide some context.

A Case for Copying

Another maybe unlikely inspiration for me was the literary critic Harold Bloom. I didn't agree with his more traditional views on the Western canon, which felt limiting and exclusionary and problematic to me. More interestingly, he wrote a book called *The Anxiety of Influence* in 1973, the year I was born, that talked about how all writers imitate their influences in one way or another, and even though it's unavoidable, they suffer anxiety in doing it. He talked, too, about how we misread or misinterpret the work of our influences, because we're all individuals. So, all said, even if you're copying someone, you end up discovering your own voice. Or at least, that's how I read it.

When I talk to artists in various fields about copying, most of them describe it as an essential part of their learning experience. "I deliberately and even slavishly copied the writing and style of writers I revered when I was figuring out how to write prose," says Dennis Cooper, "since I never studied fiction writing formally at all, not even in a workshop. By trying to copy something far away from my interests and abilities, I figured out, via what I ignored or cut out of that work, what I didn't like about fiction or think was necessary. What I wouldn't want to do in my work, even if I knew how."

While I admired authors like Pynchon, Woolf, John Barth, Stein, William Gaddis, and their large, experimental books, I was not very good at—nor really all that interested in—writing large, experimental books myself. I did try to sketch out my own version of a postmodern novel, one with a protagonist who has progeria (a genetic disorder) and who spends his days creating classical compositions based on cloud formations. It was terrible.

The process wasn't a waste, however; it made me realize I was best at keeping my material closer to home, based on my own lived experiences and true to my everyday voice. It showed me that maybe my talents weren't in inventing grandiose, baroque, imaginary worlds, and that realization helped me focus on things like curation, organization, collaboration, and simpler nonfiction writing.

Creative director Carly Ayres, who founded 100sUnder100 (a community of hundreds of creative people under a hundred years of age), points out that "copying is one of the most fundamental ways you learn anything—monkey see, monkey do. I'm still a big believer in learning by doing but have learned to create my own educational experiments." The following exercises are exactly that; a series of educational experiments to help you find your voice and purpose as you interact with the work of those you admire.

And finally, some helpful thoughts about copying from visual artist Heather Benjamin (known for her rapturous drawings of women as mythological and holy-seeming beings) to keep in mind if you're moving beyond private experiments and putting your work out into the world: "I don't think it's a great idea to go into plagiarism mode and make work that looks so much like someone else's. It's obviously even dicier if someone with a platform and an established practice is copying someone's work and then able to get it out to a big audience." Crediting your sources and linking to them or otherwise citing them is always the best practice.

"I drew *Sailor Moon* fan art when I was in fourth, fifth, and sixth grade. Those were the first obsessive line drawings I made, and I literally made hundreds of them. Sometimes I copied the original *Sailor Moon* drawings by Naoko Takeuchi. Then I moved into drawing her characters in my own poses and scenes. Eventually I made my own characters that basically just looked exactly like Takeuchi's. This was my version of 'studying the masters,' and it's still visible in what I make today."

Heather Benjamin
(Visual artist)

Study a Master

Who are your masters? Pick one work and think about how you
would do iterations of it, following the process that Heather
Benjamin describes on the facing page, when she was copying
Sailor Moon. Set three intentions and follow through.

1. An exact copy: Which work do you want to replicate,
and why?

_____

_____

_____

2. A minor variation: How can you customize or shift this
work *just slightly*, to bring a little more of yourself to it?

_____

_____

_____

_____

3. A content update: Now, adhering to the style of the
original, dig deeper to make a more thorough overhaul of the
work. What larger personal associations and content can you
employ in this next version?

_____

_____

_____

_____

Collage

Cross-pollinating your influences is an effective way to start with work that you admire and bring it to a new place, particularly if your source material is diverse. Consider these three collage-like strategies from a writer, a visual artist, and a recording artist (below); each describes taking small pieces of existing works and figuring out how to unify them in a new way. How can you translate collage to the medium of your choice?

"Looking at someone's style of painting and thinking, 'I really like this color palette, maybe I'll try working this palette or a similar one into my next piece and see how it goes,' is just part of the learning process that leads you to your own voice. I think everyone's voice is a sum of so many parts. Inevitably, by taking dismembered pieces from existing works or styles that influence you, you have to create your own new context or environment for them, which removes your work from the realm of being anything close to a carbon copy."

Heather Benjamin
(Visual artist)

"The way I started writing *Closer* was that I did cutups of six books whose writing I was really interested in (S.E. Hinton's *Rumble Fish*, Nijinsky's diary, a memoir by Paul Verlaine, and others). I constructed the voice for each chapter by mimicking the voice of one of the cutups and then gradually refined the writing away from the sources."

Dennis Cooper
(Writer, author of The George Miles Cycle,
The Sluts, *My Loose Thread*)

"Usually the 'theft' is only obvious in my mind. And I think that's because I'm copying small details in a bigger collage of small details. For example, here are my mental notes while tracking: 'I like how these Tracey Ullman backing vocals are mixed. The distortion on the synth on this one Rihanna song is cool. I like the hi-hat sound on the Thao album. Maybe I'll play a Heatmiser solo on top of the whole thing. Does the resulting song sound too much like Steely Dan?' And no one I'm working with will have any idea I was referencing any of those things."

Sadie Dupuis
(Musician, poet, solo artist,
front person of Speedy Ortiz)

Recontextualizing

"I really believe in that saying: There is nothing new under the sun. I don't think there is new content out there, there's just new lenses to filter it through, new ways of reflecting and refracting everything, ways of communicating ideas that resonate better at certain times in history than others might."

Heather Benjamin
(Visual artist)

As a kid, I loved Marcel Duchamp's concept of the readymade, where he'd take an ordinary object, like a urinal, wheel, or iron, and give it a title or reposition it by placing it in a gallery setting. In this new light, it became art. I've never been much of a visual artist, in the sense of making a painting or a sculpture. But I do know how to curate or rearrange or give a new context to something—and how to express my own point of view through the arrangement.

"Pierre Menard, Author of the Quixote" is a metafictional short story by Jorge Luis Borges. Written in the form of a scholarly review and eulogy, it analyzes the work of the fictional author Pierre Menard, who's rewritten Cervantes's *Don Quixote* word for word. The critic views Menard's work as a different, richer book because he's brought a new context to it. The real-life novelist Kathy Acker also took well-known books, like *Don Quixote*, and rewrote them from a radical female perspective. Try retyping an existing text and observe where you feel out of alignment with the voice of that work. The exercise might help you see your own context more clearly.

Make a Readymade

Choose an everyday object, and like Duchamp, turn it into art by experimenting with reframing. The goal is to defamiliarize yourself with this object, as if you are seeing it for the first time. Try moving the object into different settings, grouping it with unrelated items, or arranging multiple copies of this item. After doing this exercise, reflect on how you might use these strategies to shift the meaning of any material that you want to "steal" from others.

_____

_____

_____

_____

_____

_____

_____

_____

_____

_____

_____

_____

_____

_____

_____

"Trying to be unique
is a waste of time.
We are always unique.
The desire to be 'unique'
is tied to capitalism and
faith in oppressive fairy
tales of success and
failure in the arts."

Matthew Day Jackson
(Visual artist)

What About Uniqueness?

A discussion about copying inevitably raises the question about uniqueness as something to strive for in one's art. Interestingly, most of the artists that I've spoken to reject the idea of prioritizing uniqueness when they set out to create something. They feel that issues of uniqueness are driven by the notion that an artist must "own" something singular in their work and leverage it as a selling point. These might be useful considerations when it's time to market your art, but it's not a great headspace to be in at the start of the creative process.

"My high school yearbook featured my picture next to the superlative 'Most Unique.' That's not how 'unique' works but often how it exists in our mind. We want to think of ourselves as 'the most original.' It's an unnecessary redundancy. We are all the sum of our parts, which come from many different angles, including our experiences and every interaction we have with others. I've found that no matter what I do, my individualized voice still comes through, and to stop worrying about perceived notions of uniqueness to the audience. The most important thing is that the work is meaningful to me."

Lavender Suarez
(Musician, sound healer,
performs as C. Lavender)

"It's always been an extreme, life-or-death, if it's not totally unique it's not worth it, it's garbage, I'm a fraud ... I've always had this extreme cop in my mind at all times yelling at me that everything I do has to be original, groundbreaking, etc. I think it's held me back in a lot of ways and led me to reinvent the wheel unnecessarily.
If you're in the moment and working earnestly and honestly, I don't think uniqueness is a concern. When it comes out in a productive way, it's more a question of: How can I make this interesting? How do I make this express what I want? Instead of: How do I make this different? How do I make this stand out? Which is purely a marketing issue, concerned with monetization."

Darcie Wilder
(Writer, author of *Literally Show Me a Healthy Person*)

Michael Griffen was a violin player in the ecstatic noise duo Noggin. I met him because I dialed the phone number on the back of one of Noggin's records. I was a college sophomore at Rutgers University, doing my radio show at WRSU. This was the pre-cell phone era, and surprisingly, a crackly voice answered. Michael and I ended up speaking for about twenty minutes, and we were both laughing by the end of the call. At the time, he was in his late fifties.

We decided to do an interview for my zine, and then I booked a show for Noggin at the record store where I worked. They had some van trouble after that show, so the band stayed at my place for a couple of days. Over the years—until Michael passed away in 2008—we toured, recorded, and played music together. I also spent a lot of time at his rustic, idyllic, punk house (aka Griffenshire) in Bellingham, Washington, picking blackberries, cooking meals with friends, and talking to him about Derrida, DIY, John Cage, and life.

I was inspired by Michael's music, but I think I was more taken by the way he lived. He taught me that you can learn more from your friends than school. He also showed me a different type of rural life—one that was creatively fulfilling—and very different from the isolation of my upbringing. He even paid a portion of his bills by working on a farm, like I had as a kid. He told me he loved the freedom these decisions gave him. He modeled a positive version of the limitations I'd found stifling.

Through Michael, I saw the value of balancing work with artistic pursuits: to have a low-stress job so that you have time to do what you love. He taught me that you could grow older and not lose your ideals. When I graduated college, I had job opportunities and could have made a go as a music writer at different publications, but I didn't feel like I knew enough yet. I didn't feel wise like Michael.

I kept working at the record store, and then at Borders bookstore, so that I had time to run my label and zine and put on shows. Eventually I moved to Portland, Oregon. The city was having a moment with underground noise music, lo-fi tape labels, and experimental indie rock/pop. Also appealing was that I only knew two people who lived there. I'd spent so much of my life looking for a community, but at that moment I decided that I needed space to focus and explore. I wanted to feel a bit unmoored. Another thing Michael taught me: Don't settle too soon, or take the easy way out, or grow too comfortable.

A few years later I did go to grad school, in Buffalo. I showed up armed with so much more reading in theory and philosophy and regular life experience than I had before. I also ended up booking Noggin to play inside a large-scale installation in a gallery, and they were thankful for it. All of that because I decided to pick up the phone and call a stranger. And that stranger became a friend.

How to Find a Mentor

"Instead of cold-calling individuals asking them to be your mentor, reach out and ask them small, purposeful questions. Small questions because people are really busy, and purposeful because the other kinds are irritating. Then, let them know what you did with that answer or advice. And then do it again."

Carly Ayres
(Creative director, writer,
founder of 100sUnder100)

"I would encourage young artists to reach out and ask for support from artists they admire, but with the understanding that a lot of artists are self-involved and that a nonresponse means nothing about the quality of their own work."

Dennis Cooper
(Writer, author of The George Miles Cycle,
The Sluts, My Loose Thread)

"Just observe. If one must have a mentor, observe from as far away as you can. As I write this, I imagine myself in the woods in the dark and Willie Nelson is way ahead of me and he has a light. I cannot find his path, but I know where he is. I have to find my own path if I am to hear him play by the campfire."

Matthew Day Jackson
(Visual artist)

"I realize now my greatest mentors are dead writers, because I feel a responsibility to carry on in the tradition they imparted to all of us."

Patty Yumi Cottrell
(Writer, author of *Sorry to Disrupt the Peace*)

Reaching Out

Try to dispense with the conventional idea of what a mentorship should be. As Carly Ayres admits, "For so long, I had this idea of mentorship being some sort of contract where two individuals agree to embark on this glorious journey together, one with regular check-ins and milestones along the way to career nirvana. And while that may very well exist, mine have been far more organic. Usually a self-initiated coffee chat led to another, to another, and so on."

Approach someone you admire for a list of recommendations or some advice on how this person does their thing. Who could you reach out to, and what are your specific asks?

_____

_____

_____

_____

_____

_____

_____

_____

_____

_____

_____

What creative works have served as mentors to you?
Make a list of a few books, movies, visual art, etc.

Mutual Benefit

Reaching out to someone you admire might result in a recommendation or a tip, a mentorship, a lifelong friendship, or maybe something significant that you'll never know anything about. Writer Hermione Hoby has a lot to say on the benefits of hearing from her readers: "I'm always astonished to hear from anyone who's read my book; I just can't really believe that anyone out there's read it. The thing about being a writer is that you work in private and are appreciated (or not) in private. This is incredibly special, there's a sort of purity to it, but it also means most writers have very little sense of their audience."

She had an opportunity to express her enthusiasm to one of her own heroes, but she almost didn't say anything. Here's what happened: "Several years ago, Mary Gaitskill sat down next to me on an Amtrak train back to New York. Her novels had shaped me so much as a young woman. So naturally I froze, sick with paralysis. Do I tell her? I had to tell her! But how to tell her? Finally, as Penn Station came into our sights, I swallowed and said something. She looked utterly startled. She said, stricken, and with this extraordinary intensity: 'Really?' And then, looking right at me, she said: 'I was thinking of giving up.'"

While Hermione wouldn't claim that this chance exchange on the train is what kept Mary Gaitskill writing, her takeaway is clear: "There are so many people who, to me, are canonical, godlike, but I strongly suspect that to themselves they are just their wearisome selves, making coffee and picking up their dog's shit and sighing as they sit down at their laptop again." Regardless of past or current successes, people need to be reminded of their impact.

I've been lucky to find several mentors who were older and far more established than I was, but who readily claimed that they were also learning something from me. Dennis Cooper says: "I always try to treat other artists, whatever point they're at in their development, as peers. And the truth is, I learn a lot from reading the work of artists who are still developing because the talent and promise are very exciting in and of themselves. So I inherently see that kind of mentor relationship as a two-way street, where I'm getting as much out of it as they are."

As I mentioned previously, my relationship with Dennis began with a fan letter, which led to doing my graduate school thesis on his writing. Eventually, I worked on his archive at New York University, edited an anthology in which he and Eileen Myles wrote the afterword, and now he's a contributor to this book. When you find a mentor, think about what you bring to the equation and offer help where you can. There is reciprocity in these relationships, even when the hero or mentor would seem to have more resources or clout.

"It's a pleasure as well as a duty to help other artists. This is how art works—through influence, reciprocity, inspiration. We all need each other. I think being truly, sincerely curious about someone's work is one of the best gifts to give. When someone feels they are being taken seriously as an artist, it gives them permission to take themselves seriously."

Hermione Hoby
(Writer, critic, author of
Neon in Daylight, *Virtue*)

Who Can You Help?

Inside the circles on this page, write down the names of
people whose creativity you can encourage. This could mean
asking them about their work, introducing them to someone,
or doing a small favor that frees them up in some way.
Color in each circle as you reach out.

Conclusion

There are infinite reasons why you might be influenced by someone else's art, and just as many ways to apply this influence in your own work. You might be influenced through a misunderstanding of what someone else is doing. While writing his 1957 novel, *On the Road*, Jack Kerouac fed a 120-foot roll of architect's paper through his typewriter as a way of keeping his thoughts flowing. As a kid, I thought he'd also written that book in one take, so I tried to write that way. There was much more editing and revision (and helping hands) on his side than I'd realized, but my misunderstanding of that process taught me to write quickly, without stalling or leaning on artifice. My work felt more honest to me.

You don't need to agree with, or be inspired by, everything that someone else does to be influenced by them. Many of my influences and mentors were important role models through their way of making things, not because of what they made. Again, the Beat poets come to mind. It wasn't their writing I liked; I thought a lot of it was cheesy. What I admired was the spirit of what they were doing, or what I imagined them to be doing, and the community they created while doing it. I liked the idea of wandering and collaborating.

Copying someone else is encoded in how we learn, but it can be an uncomfortable stage in the creative process. It's useful to keep tuning into and refining why you are drawn to someone else's work. Nika Roza Danilova, who makes dark but uplifting music under the name Zola Jesus, has found an interesting evolution in her motive for copying: "Whenever I tried to copy someone I realized I couldn't do it, or it came off insincere and sort of tacky. It was easier to copy an attitude or a feeling. I do that still sometimes when I feel like I need to go someplace that doesn't exist within my own set of experiences or current attitude."

Here are some ways to lean into your influences and find your own voice in the process:

> Think about the range of things that you have liked over time, even before your taste gelled to its current state. Can you use bits and pieces of these diverse influences in your work?

> Apply your own content—your specific point of view and experiences—to the styles and forms that you admire. Keep referring back to your reflections in Chapter 1.

> Write a heartfelt fan letter. It could be a means of articulating what you hope to engage, accomplish, or exemplify in your own work.

> Look for mentors everywhere and reach out with specific questions. You may get a response! If not, are you any worse off for trying?

> Remember that you can have influence as well. You'll feel more secure asking for help when you are aware of how you can help others, too—even if the gesture seems small.

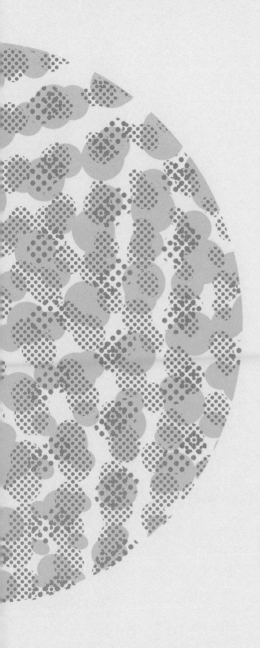

"The world is a really interesting place, and making art is a way of being in the world. I don't really know how else to be. It's a stance of curiosity."

Sarah Gerard
(Writer, author of *Binary Star, Sunshine State, True Love*)

In this chapter, you'll tune into the things that intrigue you and see where doing research takes you. Feeling inspired is exciting, but it's not a prerequisite for creativity. I've generated so much more by following my curiosity than I would have if I'd waited to feel inspired.

It might seem easier to land on one "signature" thing and to keep doing just that, but I've always preferred pushing myself, even if that means floundering for a bit. It can feel like I'm doing more research than actively making, but I see it as all part of the same process: Making things is ongoing research, and research is part of the art.

So if you connect with something, try researching that subject thoroughly. You may go down a fork in the road and come back with things you weren't expecting to find. It's exciting not knowing exactly where you'll end up, and ideas often arrive in detours.

The flip side of doing research is that you can get over-whelmed with information or examples of what's already been done. Or you may not know when to stop. Part of your practice will be pausing from research and allowing your own vision or imagination to take over.

Also look for some relationships between things that catch your attention. Your specific constellation of interests contains unique connections, and this is where creative possibilities lie.

Curiosity and Research

Part of growing up pre-Internet (I didn't have a computer until I went to college) meant my path was a little weird, as most paths of curious kids were then. I didn't have Wikipedia to direct me through a band's entire album catalogue. I had to piece things together in my own particular timeline.

I used the few cassettes and albums I owned as tiny, self-contained resources. I'd read the liner notes of a Sonic Youth album and discover Raymond Carver that way. I looked to see whose art it was on the cover of Sonic Youth's album *Daydream Nation* and discovered Gerhardt Richter. Or it just came down to listening—I learned about Keats and Yeats through the Smiths' song "Cemetery Gates" and Jack Kerouac (and the Beats) via 10,000 Maniacs' song "Hey Jack Kerouac."

I discovered Andy Warhol through some of his work at the Philadelphia Museum of Art. Then, once I could drive, I learned more about him. At the public library, I picked up *The Andy Warhol Diaries* and then tried to research each person he mentioned. I failed, but I did learn about Lou Reed and the Velvet Underground that way.

The "local library" was about forty minutes from my place, but I drove there at least once a week and camped out until I was able to make some sort of connection. My resources were scarce, and so I never felt overwhelmed. I'd arrive at the library with a specific question and stay until I had it solved (or close to solved), and then hop back in the car with the books I needed and read them at home. If new questions arose, I'd address them at the library the next week.

When I was living in Canada in my early twenties, I wasn't legally allowed to work, so I started pawning my belongings and reading deeply at the public library each day as if it was my full-time job. I used that time to get through Proust, Flaubert, Kafka, Woolf, Goethe, etc. I'd take out records, too, which is how I learned about classical music. Once I was able to get a job, I found an assistant's position at the Southern Alberta Art Gallery. I was tasked with filing all of the art magazines in the gallery's library, which is how I discovered my eventual friend and collaborator Matthew Barney's work. Again, research.

When you move step-by-step through a subject, you learn that subject thoroughly. Research, in its various forms, has helped me start to make connections between the things that interested me and to better understand specifically *why* they spoke to me. It's helped me to develop my specific taste across genres (visual art, music, literature). It's exposed me to new forms and ideas. It also gave me my own very particular aesthetic, something that I came to on my own via years of trial and error.

Of course, research doesn't just mean reading books— it can also be about building or taking something apart to see how it works, or making daily observations, or doing experiments. Sometimes, it just means paying close attention.

Curiosity and Research

Inventory of Likes

Make a few different lists of things that you like by following
the prompts below. Go with your gut—this isn't a "top ten" list.
Do try to be specific about each thing (not "apples," but rather
"honey crisp apples; grandma's favorite, too"). In other words,
attempt to capture the essence of why you like something—
or the quality you are drawn to—as well.

Things I Liked as a Child

1. _____
2. _____
3. _____
4. _____
5. _____
6. _____
7. _____
8. _____
9. _____
10. _____

Cultural Artifacts* I Like

1. _____
2. _____
3. _____
4. _____
5. _____
6. _____

*paintings/images, songs, films, books, buildings, video games

7. _____

8. _____

9. _____

10. _____

Things I Like to Do**

1. _____

2. _____

3. _____

4. _____

5. _____

6. _____

7. _____

8. _____

9. _____

10. _____

Anything I Liked This Week

1. _____

2. _____

3. _____

4. _____

5. _____

6. _____

7. _____

8. _____

9. _____

10. _____

**any activity that gives you some pleasure: folding laundry, doing crosswords, playing the guitar, writing poetry

"I consider my work research-based, but it doesn't tend to start there. I'm usually first captivated by a relationship between several things. I might come upon this reading or in conversation. I spend some time drawing and trying to map out a form or a space between the elements in the relationship. Then I start the research. I'm either not a very good researcher, or else I'm not interested in learning too much about any one element in the relationship. I'm ultimately more interested in the form that binds them."

Matthew Barney
(Multimedia artist, creator
of *The Cremaster Cycle*)

Matthew Barney is known for elaborately produced art films and expansive sculptural installations. His projects include creating music from the sound of bees mixed with heavy metal drumbeats and vocals, choreographing elaborate dances in football fields, and staging hardcore bands in the Guggenheim Museum. He directs his films, acts in them, and builds the sets.

Matthew was born in the Bay Area, but spent the bulk of his childhood and adolescence in rural Idaho, where he quarter-backed his high school football team. He went to Yale University, planning to go pre-med, and modeled for J.Crew to help pay his tuition. He also played for Yale's football team, but had to quit because the National College Athletic Association prohibited paid modeling.

While an undergraduate at Yale, Matthew began focusing on art. His first works involved him scaling the Yale gymnasium walls, often nude, in feats of pure athleticism. These led to his *Drawing Restraint* series, which finds him battling against an impediment of some sort (an elastic band, rope, hockey skates, a trampoline, etc.) while attempting to draw on a wall or a ceiling or other surface.

In 2003, Matthew mounted a site-specific takeover of the Guggenheim Museum to feature *The Cremaster Cycle*, his series of five feature-length art films. With photographs, drawings, sculptures, and the films themselves, he created a densely layered mythology drawing thematically from biology, athletic competition, and ideas about transformation and potential. All of this comes from his own unique web of influences, expressed in forms that he was singularly interested in exploring.

Connect the Dots

Take a look at your Inventory of Likes on page 90. Some of the entries will be logically related, and others might make less sense grouped together at first glance. Can you imagine bringing the most unlikely elements together in one creative project? What would your Guggenheim Museum takeover look like?

How Do You Research?

"In the last few years, I have been going to a lot of estate sales, which feels like endless research. The sales are in the individual's home, so it's like you are walking into their autobiography or a museum of personal objects."

Beth Campbell
(Visual artist)

"Sometimes I get spurred from a conversation, quote, or an image and I just want to explore it. I'll get so deep into researching and completely forget what I want to accomplish in the first place. It's been a process to recognize that it's OK and actually strengthens my work."

Shanekia McIntosh
(Poet, performer, artist, librarian)

"A type of research is simply putting yourself near things that inspire you, like going to look at art or watching stand-up. It doesn't have to speak to your project directly. You're just letting your lizard brain make the connections."

Ling Ma
(Writer, critic, teacher,
author of *Severance*)

"I love getting down to the many-tabbed, open-book, magnifying glass on YouTube brand of research. But my eyes are opened in the most unique and exciting ways when I'm not in front of a computer screen. And so that tells me that the world is waiting for me to engage with it in a way that enlivens the work."

Hanif Abdurraqib
(Poet, writer, author of *They Can't
Kill Us Until They Kill Us*,
A Fortune for Your Disaster,
and *Go Ahead in the Rain*)

Reading the Credits

Pick a work of art that is significant to you and research what it's absorbed and harnessed from history by following up on its references. Research the makers, the context (place and period it was made), and all of the references within the piece. Make a catalog of things to follow up on, and check them off as you research them. Maybe write them out like the credits at the end of a film—who and what contributed to this work of art?

☐ _____

☐ _____

☐ _____

☐ _____

☐ _____

☐ _____

☐ _____

☐ _____

☐ _____

☐ _____

☐ _____

☐ _____

☐ _____

☐ _____

☐ _____

"Everything is a product of your inputs and experiences. So the best way to make original work is to diversify those inputs. Surround yourself with different people doing different things, read new books, consume a range of content. Go against the grain. When they zig, roll on the floor. The only way to ensure originality is to apply your unique combination of experiences and skills. It's the only variable no one else possesses."

Carly Ayres
(Creative director, writer, founder of 100sUnder100)

Diversify Your Inputs

Think about ways to counterbalance your dominant interests, activities, or point of view. This could be as simple as taking a different route to work or listening to the news from a different media source. Or maybe researching the opposite of what you like.* Record your thoughts after trying one of these strategies (or list some things you'd like to try to diversify your inputs).

_____

_____

_____

_____

_____

_____

_____

_____

_____

_____

_____

_____

_____

_____

_____

*For example, if you love Victorian houses, look into Brutalist architecture.

"A moment. A glint in someone's eye, seeing a squirrel eating a bird, the scent of a museum I went to as a child—it only takes a fraction of a second for something to make an impression. These moments make their way into lyrics, poems, videos."

Ioanna Gika
(Musician, solo artist, actor)

Research can be as basic as daily observation. It's not difficult to cultivate an art of noticing, of simply paying attention. For example, something I do now and then is to ask my kids to look around the room in our house or some other familiar place, and point out a few things to me that they've never noticed before—a shape in a plaster molding, a mark on the floor, a pattern on the side of a lampshade. It's interesting to watch familiar things defamiliarize and then come back into view.

There's a tendency toward overstimulation in modern life, and it's easy to succumb to information overload. Sarah Gerard, a novelist and essayist whose work is heavily research-based, knows this feeling well: "Because I'm a curious person by nature and am perhaps more dopamine-motivated than some other people, I can easily spend hours just clicking and scrolling and clicking and scrolling. I find this mentally and spiritually draining, so for my overall wellness, I know I need boundaries around it."

How, in the present, can you try to instill those sorts of boundaries or limits? The problem with an endless scroll is that it tends to flatten information, and it's easier to forget. It's essential to find effective ways to digest what you're consuming. What if you punctuate your research with a meditative stroll? Maybe try reading for forty-five minutes and then going to a local park to think about what you just read. Or, on your lunch break, take a notebook instead of your phone.

Also, when does the research or work stop feeling useful and start feeling like unproductive procrastination? It's hard to nail down an exact moment. For me, I do background work, pile up ideas, then suddenly I want to move forward immediately. When that happens, I feel like one of those bucking horses at a rodeo, jumping in place behind the closed gate. The second it opens, I'm out the shoot. Pay attention to your own signs that you have enough input for now.

Personally, I always find more inspiration by unplugging and taking a fifteen-minute walk than I will doing an Internet search for the same amount of time. When I walk to work, I don't look at my phone or listen to music. I notice things about my environment—something as simple as the way shadows were cast on a sidewalk through spring blossoms on a tree—and connect them to my memories and emotions. They come back later in my writing, curation, and art projects.

Think of small things you can do in your day-to-day to make room for this kind of open-ended reflection.

Curiosity and Research

For one week, make one observation at a set time in the day.
Write it down. It doesn't need to be huge or time-consuming.
In fact, tuning into smaller things can be especially useful.*

MONDAY   DATE:____ /____ /____ TIME: ____:____

TUESDAY   DATE:____ /____ /____ TIME: ____:____

WEDNESDAY   DATE:____ /____ /____ TIME: ____:____

---

*What if you look out the same window of your home each day and catalog what you see. What changes?
What stays the same? Think about how the weather and light quality shift the colors of the buildings; maybe
even snap a photo so you can look back over time and see these differences.

THURSDAY   DATE:____ /____ /____ TIME: ____:____

FRIDAY   DATE:____ /____ /____ TIME: ____:____

SATURDAY   DATE:____ /____ /____ TIME: ____:____

SUNDAY   DATE:____ /____ /____ TIME: ____:____

"I have worked in book production, at an indie feminist magazine, a men's lifestyle magazine, a gelato shop, a library, a social media start-up, and a financial communications group. And I always felt, every time I began a new job, that I would somehow disappear into that role, that I would take on a new identity. For a long time, I felt like a voyeur in my own life as I infiltrated different industries. When I wrote more fiction, I began to see many of my past jobs as a kind of research, even if I didn't know it at the time. In *Severance*, the job that Candace Chen worked was one that I had done, too, in a slightly different capacity."

Ling Ma
(Writer, critic, teacher, author of *Severance*)

Your Creative Resumé

Think about how your past and present work experiences may have affected your own creative work. Were they unexpected research? Make a list of each job you've worked, and beneath each job title, list something you learned from it or learned about yourself from it.

"I have faith in meandering."

Beth Campbell

(Visual artist)

The word "research" can be intimidating, causing flashbacks to book reports written at the last minute in grade school. But research is something we're always doing, even if we're not totally aware of it. You stumble on something interesting and Google it. That's research. You hear one song, then find more songs by that same artist. This is research, too.

There's so much creative potential in simply being "interested." You don't need to be "obsessed" or "passionate" about a topic you're researching. Some ambivalence on a subject might actually be useful: It shows an openness to new information and other points of view.

My friend Dominick Fernow went to design school and studied typography, but ended up becoming a noise and electronic musician with hundreds of releases to his name. For years, he owned an influential record store in Manhattan and now curates an annual festival focused around his record label. He's published books, too. All to say, Dominick has a lot of interests! He told me this story once, and it's stuck with me:

> "When I first moved to New York City, an old friend of mine, Matt Kenny, said to me: 'I've realized that I don't have a lot of interests . . . basically, I'm just interested in one thing, and that's painting.' It sounds grandiose in a way, but it was a radical position. Rather than saying, 'I'm obsessed or driven by my subject,' it's more of an eliminationist way of putting devotion to an art practice."*

*Stosuy, Brandon, "Musician and artist Dominick Fernow on making what you can't find," The Creative Independent, August 23, 2018.

We're told that we should follow our passions, which can make it hard to prioritize something that we are merely "interested in." It's tricky making time for unpaid work that many people may consider a hobby. It helps, maybe, if you get rid of the idea of "hobbies" and instead consider whatever you do—whether it pays or not—as something worth doing in and of itself. It's good to acknowledge to yourself that diving into something is worthwhile simply because you're interested in it.

Digging into your interests may evolve into a passion project or draw you into scenes previously unknown. Or you'll just learn something and move on. Either way, following your curiosity needs no further justification. Here are some different ways to engage it:

> Get your research muscles working by doing a deep dive into one work of art that you love. Make note of any new curiosities that come up.
> Look at the variety of things that you like and pay extra attention to the oddballs. Your personal taste and point of view can be defined by how you synthesize the diversity of your interests.
> What does research look like for you? Is it wandering through shopping centers, making observations while on the job, or listening to your friends talk?
> Give yourself time to digest what you're researching and to connect with it on an emotional and personal level. This is basic advice, but going for a walk and bringing a notebook really helps.

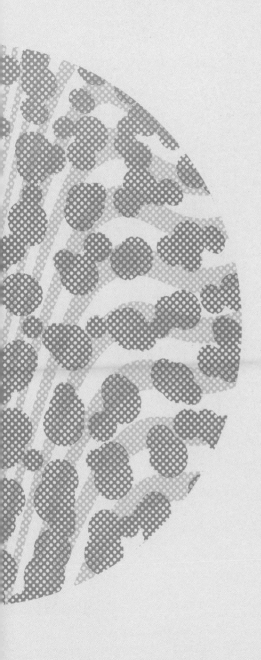

"There's not much nobility in throwing out all the interesting progress that's been made by other people, and it's a part of being in a community: building on each other's work, collaborating. Ego makes this harder because it's always keeping score of where ideas came from."

Darcie Wilder
(Writer, author of *Literally Show Me a Healthy Person*)

In this chapter, you'll think about how community and collaborations can make your work stronger. Collaboration is not about steamrolling others with your own ideas; it involves being open to possibilities. Community is about being open to others in general. You show up, support, and give back.

Making work is a day-by-day process, and it's hard to go it alone. As musician and professor Drew Daniel explains, "Some days you love your own work, and some days it seems like garbage and you feel like a failure. Other people can help you check yourself against these excesses in both directions. We need other people to know ourselves, and we need other people to know our work."

Some art practices require that the artist spend a lot of time by themselves. In this situation, how does one balance a solitary pursuit with connecting with others and sharing their work? Other artists' projects are inherently collaborative and community-based. In these cases, it's worth unpacking how collaborations come about and what makes them work.

Collaborating and engaging with a community are areas where ego can be challenged. Letting go of ego is easier said than done. But there can be enormous payoff in finding outlets to share your work (and share resources), receiving honest feedback, and creating something stronger than you could on your own.

"You can't share something that you haven't committed to making."

Kevin Beasley
(Visual artist, 2020 finalist
for the Hugo Boss Award)

Kevin Beasley's 2018 Whitney Museum exhibition, *A view of a landscape*, involved family and American history, found objects, assemblage, sound design, installation, and performance. His meditation on making and sharing work (below) brings up fundamental questions for every artmaker:

"As an artist, I feel we have two big decisions to make. The first decision is whether you should make art or not. Is making art your way of thinking about complex ideas, and is it the only way you can engage in the world? Or is artmaking just another profession that you can make money doing? Is being an artist about being popular within a specific culture? If you're the type of artist who needs to be making art—that there isn't any other way of being in the world—then that tells you a lot about how you value your process.

The second decision has to come second—it cannot come first—and that decision is whether or not you will share your art with others. For an artist to make art and not share it doesn't mean they aren't an artist. It just means they aren't concerned with their work reaching other people.

The decision to share your art is one that gets you thinking about audience; who do I share this work with? Context; where should my work exist and be seen? Within that, sharing the work at different stages of its completion and exposing the process is one that has so many decisions within it, all concerned with levels of comfort, discomfort, vulnerability, and confidence.

If you take these two decisions seriously and consider the nuances of each and every single day you go to the studio, I believe you'll grow as an artist and as a person."

Christopher Y. Lew, the curator for Kevin's Whitney show, noted to me that "some [artists] focus on what they make in the studio and think less about how it comes together in a gallery as an exhibition. Others know exactly how their pieces should be arranged for the viewing public." Think about where you fall on in this spectrum. Is your work context-specific, and do you want to shape the conditions in which it is seen, heard, or discovered? How much, and when, do you want to engage other people in your practice?

Regardless, it's critical you stay grounded in why *you*'re making something because, truthfully, you might be the only one who cares about your work. Also, you don't want to fall into the trap of allowing external voices to derail what's internally driving you. You really don't have an obligation to share the work, and maybe not everything should be shared. You're an artist either way.

Community and Collaboration

Your Reasons for Sharing

Reflecting on the previous passage by Kevin Beasley, write about why you are making work and whether it's important to you to share it. How vulnerable do you feel about putting your work out there?

_____

_____

_____

_____

_____

_____

_____

_____

_____

_____

_____

_____

_____

_____

_____

_____

_____

Critical Timing

Singer-songwriter Jess Williamson has figured out what she needs when sharing an early version of a piece: "The truth is, if I'm sending a demo to a friend, I don't want any critical feedback. I really just want them to be encouraging. But if we are collaborating, it means I trust the person and respect their ideas, and so I do want their input." When you share a work in progress, be deliberate about both the timing and type of response you're looking for:

"I feel protective over the early drafts of my work. In my undergraduate years I was making large layered paintings, and a fellow student used to come into my studio when I had just made the first mark and say, 'It's done!' It felt taunting—that's not the type of painter I was or the type of paintings I was interested in making. That's when I started to understand that not all feedback is helpful, and it's on me to discern what feedback I really sit with, and what doesn't serve me."

Annie Bielski
(Visual artist, writer)

"When I'm reaching out for criticism, the feedback I'm asking for is usually to confirm something I've been suspicious of. I tend to take it on quickly and want to discuss. However, in a broader sense—the general population's criticism of finished work is something I've had to make peace with. Knowing too much positivity or negativity about one's work can be destructive. I have been hyperaware of, or engaged with criticisms in the past, and have seen it affect the honesty of my output."

George Clarke
(Musician, photographer,
vocalist of Deafheaven)

Drew Daniel is a tenured professor at Johns Hopkins University and an electronic musician in the band Matmos. He's written books both on the English Renaissance and on the industrial group Throbbing Gristle. Below, he discusses different ways he responds to feedback, depending on the forum and medium of the work. Think about this in regard to your own output: Are you more receptive to feedback in some areas of your life than others? What can you learn from the instances where you're more open?

"I take criticism of my academic writing very badly, generally: I'm waspish and defensive and thin-skinned, and it's very awkward. The problem is that, as the slogan goes, 'writing is rewriting.' If you aren't folding that into your process, your work will suffer. But emotionally, it's very difficult for me to seek and receive feedback on academic writing.

As far as writing about music or making music goes, it's like a different, less-fraught part of my brain is operating. With music, you try things out in performance with audiences, and part of you is figuring out what the crowd resonates with, but part of it is just that you hear your own work with a new kind of nakedness and clarity when you're in the middle of present-ing it to others. Do you feel ashamed of it? Do you feel proud? Does it need something that you didn't notice before? The vulnerability teaches you what the form has and what it lacks, I think. Maybe your capacity for self-critique kicks in when you're in the presence of other people?"

Self-Critique

How do you react to feedback—particularly criticism? Is your instinct to argue against it or to take it onboard quickly, or do you sit with it and try not to react? Can you think of any areas of your life where you are able to turn feedback into a useful form of self-critique?

The Collaborative Practice

For a lot of what I do, I work alone. I've joked with friends that in this setting I can sometimes feel like Forrest Gump bouncing from one thing to the next without a specific goal in mind, but I manage to keep bouncing anyhow. Most of my momentum comes from collaboration. Joining forces with someone else is a useful and practical form of inspiration, one that can offer relief from working entirely on your own terms, constrained by the limitations of your own skill set.

One of my longest-running collaborations has been with artist Matthew Barney, who I met in 2006 when I interviewed him for *The Believer*. We were introduced by a mutual friend, Drew Daniel, connected over a conversation about heavy metal, and decided to see a band together a few days later. It was a quick and natural friendship. Matthew and I have similar quiet demeanors and ridiculous senses of humor, and the laughs came easy and frequent. We also soon learned that we worked well together on projects.

Almost fifteen years later, we've produced art books, zines, and dozens of semi-public events at a warehouse space in Long Island City we call REMAINS. These events started as a way to take a break from our "more serious," maybe more stressful, individual projects. We saw them as ways to test ideas for things we'd want to do again later in more institutional settings.

Reflecting back now, we've never once had a major disagreement, even when working on incredibly complicated builds. We can go from goofy to intensely focused and back again in a minute. We're both practical, efficient, and don't like to waste time with small talk or overly long meetings. Also, we don't keep track of whose idea is whose.

When I asked people about collaboration for this book, I approached Matthew, and this is what he said: "You have a way of trusting your instincts and mobilizing ideas quickly without shutting down the possibility for the ideas to change as the project is realized. This creates a flow, and I've learned a lot from your approach."

I've learned from him, too. I'm not someone who makes art. Matthew is used to envisioning and executing large-scale artworks. He often takes lead on the technical side of the projects. If I was working with anyone other than Matthew, there's no way I'd imagine pulling off a dance piece involving a live horse or an amateur wrestling match choreographed to noise.

Even the most organically formed partnerships benefit from having a motto or a consciously articulated phrase for the ideals that you share. Over the years, Matthew and I have come up with personal slogans that we say to each other when working on a project. One of these, "Blood Pattern Form," is connected to sports, training, and developing a ritual. You put your heart into the project, you develop a pattern and a system, and throughout, you always maintain your form. These ideas are personal and meaningful to us, and they keep us going.

Why Do You Collaborate?

"I love collaboration. It frees you from self-consciousness. You have this stimulus of what the other person has just produced, and you play off one another. You can subvert it, you can extend it, you can take it in a direction suggested by one word in it. You get out of yourself."

Richard Hell
(Writer, poet, musician,
author of *Godlike*, *Go Now*, and
the album *Blank Generation*)[*]

"I draw strength and inspiration and fear from the presence of others. The fear part is that I don't want to disappoint people or seem to have brought something weak to the table. The presence of others means that the possibility of failure is real, and that motivates you."

Drew Daniel
(Musician, writer, Johns Hopkins
University professor, member of
Matmos, performs as Soft Pink Truth)

[*]Stosuy, Brandon, "Richard Hell on collaboration," The Creative Independent, November 28, 2017.

"Sometimes I can see an idea more clearly when it comes out of someone else's mouth than I can when it sputters out of my own brain."

Vernon Chatman
(Comedy writer, actor, producer, *South Park*, *The Shivering Truth*)

"The beauty to me is finding people that are searching for the same outcome and then building our project around intention. Are we setting out to have fun, make art, build community? Hopefully all three."

JD Samson
(Musician, NYU professor, member of Le Tigre, cofounder of MEN and Crickets)

"Find people with whom you can practice mutual self-delusion. There are limits to how far you alone can deceive yourself into devotion to an idea. The right partner gets you further in before goddamn reality regains the upper hand."

Vernon Chatman
(Comedy writer, actor, producer, *South Park*, *The Shivering Truth*)

"One of the most important parts of finding a collaborator is admitting what you can't do well and finding someone that can do that better. There is a lot of peace within the concept of trusting that they will do a great job and allowing yourself more time for what you are good at. I love when people allow me to do what I do best. I feel trusted. What we have in common is a desire to support each other to get things done. To push through. To process. To make art again and again and again."

JD Samson
(Musician, NYU professor,
member of Le Tigre,
cofounder of MEN and Crickets)

The Balance Sheet

Consider your creative practice. Make one list of things that
you enjoy and are good at doing. Make a second list of things
that you think would be handled better by someone else. Let
this be your guide when looking for a collaborator.

My Strengths   My Partner's Strengths

_____   _____

_____   _____

_____   _____

_____   _____

_____   _____

_____   _____

_____   _____

_____   _____

_____   _____

_____   _____

_____   _____

_____   _____

_____   _____

_____   _____

_____   _____

Desert Island DJ Set

For years, Björk and I organized an annual DJ set. We'd choose a day, usually in May, and ask friends to DJ with us. These events were either benefits or they were free, and they took place in a variety of spaces: a parking garage, a bookstore, a warehouse, clubs, galleries, bars. They celebrated the start of summer, and the idea was to get people together to share music and dance. We'd usually pick a theme—basslines, hand-claps, joy—and often invited people who never DJ'd before (like our friend Alex Ross, who covers classical music for *The New Yorker*) to try to work that idea into their set.

People often ask, "If you were having a dinner party and could invite anyone, living or dead, who would you invite?" Or, "If you were stuck on an island, which five albums would you want to have with you?" I think it's more interesting to ask "If you were to choose five people to collaborate on an event with you, who would they be?" What would each person bring to the event? Maybe they just make you happy, or maybe they have a legitimate skill. This is a good way to think closely about your community and who you'd like to bring together into one space. So many of my collaborative projects have begun from this very straightforward starting point.

The Five

Choose five people in your life that you'd like to bring together, potentially to create something. You don't need to be clear on what the project is; just list the players and their particular gifts.

1. _____

_____

_____

2. _____

_____

_____

3. _____

_____

_____

4. _____

_____

_____

5. _____

_____

_____

Tricking the Ego

A fruitful collaboration isn't necessarily going to be effortless and free-flowing. Some artists feel that an element of competition in a partnership compels them to bring their best ideas to the table. Maybe for you, collaboration is an opportunity to surrender control of just one aspect of the creative process, or to invite a carefully selected X factor. Here, comedy writer Vernon Chatman and musician Drew Daniel, both of whom I've collaborated with, describe how they work with others to get a little bit beyond and outside of themselves:

"Your work expands when you open the door to other people, and it can be scary because you lose that 'control freak' persona, but you gain something, too. In my experience, you get a lot more out of what your work can do when you collaborate and stay loose. But maybe I'm being a hypocrite here, because I also edit the living shit out of whatever people send to me, so maybe this is an illusion and I'm the same old control freak?"

Drew Daniel
(Musician, writer, Johns Hopkins professor, member of Matmos, performs as Soft Pink Truth)

"Find people smarter than you and aspire to be smarter than them. A great partner inspires you to anticipate what they are going to say—and makes it so your guess is something better than what you would have come up with on your own. That way, even if they do happen to say some dumb shit, you can still use what you thought they were going to add. And you can pretend it was your idea when, secretly, it actually was. It is truly best if you can't remember who came up with what—that you have surrendered your egos to the project."

Vernon Chatman
(Comedy writer, actor, producer, *South Park*, *The Shivering Truth*)

When I was in grad school, I became interested in a "scene" of writers—Dennis Cooper, Kevin Killian, Dodie Bellamy, Robert Glück, and others—loosely associated with the New Narrative movement launched in the Bay Area in the late seventies. More importantly, to me at least, they seemed to be connected based on shared philosophies of life and friendship. I decided to propose an academic conference that would bring together this largely West Coast poetic community with writers gathered around the University of Buffalo.

I went to grad school without any intention of remaining in academia. I'd been looking for people to talk to about books, and I wanted some structure around what I was reading. While I was there, I continued to put on shows, play in bands, and work outside jobs. I had never organized an academic conference before, and I wanted this event to be accessible and draw in people from a variety of backgrounds.

I ended up putting together Prose Acts, a hybrid arts festival that included discussion panels, readings, and live music performances that took place in venues around the community. Eileen Myles curated a series of events involving Mary Gaitskill, Anohni, Douglas A. Martin, and Michelle Tea, among others. The National opened for Dennis Cooper's reading. These happenings felt celebrational, brimming with energy, and even raucous at times.

I decided to organize Prose Acts largely because I was excited by the work I was reading and I felt like I'd understand it more if I met the people behind it. Reaching out to these people and connecting the dots between different writers felt like an independent study.

And as mentioned, I wasn't interested in the inaccessible aspects of graduate school (the jargon, the elitism), which I found depressing and uninspiring. Prose Acts was my way to contribute and to join together the different Buffalo communities I inhabited: music, university, art, a variety of random friends. It felt necessary to my survival in the city.

Not all of it was great. It was the first time I requested funding, which prepared me for a future of complicated grant forms and applications. It was also the first time I encountered institutional territorialism. I was careful to include old-school tenured academics and younger upstarts and different types of organizations. I tried to make sure that no one felt left out, but people still felt left out. I learned, too, that this is unavoidable.

Most importantly, Prose Acts cemented in my mind that you shouldn't be afraid to try to invent new forms, and it led me to be increasingly experimental and multidisciplinary in the curatorial work I did. Projects and collaborations don't exist in a vacuum, and they don't have to end when they're over. Prose Acts took place in 2001, and twenty years later, I'm still in close conversation with many of the people who participated in it. We've since collaborated on other events, contributed to each other's books, and made art together. I could not have expected that the community would be so ongoing. These connections continue, and continue to grow deeper.

Creating a community, an audience, and a scene is something I've been oriented toward for decades at this point. Bringing people together is central to my creative practice. But in speaking with different artists, I've seen how community is variously defined, particularly in relation to their process:

"My communities have never been so much for career or collaborations," says visual artist and visual director Shawna X, "but more so ones that have deep, personal roots focused on the connection of emotion, experience, understanding. Everyone is vastly different in their careers and outlook on life, and I love how these differences in their daily experience expand my own perspectives and growth in my personal and creative path."

Visual artist Kevin Beasley keeps an intimate circle for discussing work: "I'm constantly in conversation with just a few people about work and the process. It's invigorating, and I wish there was more of it, but many folks that I love to talk to have full plates, as do I, so it's about being totally present in the conversations when they're happening, because it may be a while before it happens again."

Drew Daniel's work as a musician and academic has pulled him into diverse communities and spaces: "You find your people by looking around, going to things, keeping your eyes and ears open. For me, it started when I started hanging out at a record store and talking to the clerk, and then tagging along with friends to a punk show in a basement at a church. But there are online communities of scholars of Renaissance literature that I found on Twitter and I 'know' them even though I've never been face-to-face with some of them."

The Widening Circle

Use these concentric circles to visualize your community. Those who support you the most intimately go in the center. The larger circles are for groups, schools, organizations, and other scenes that you follow. How far into this world would you like to share your work?

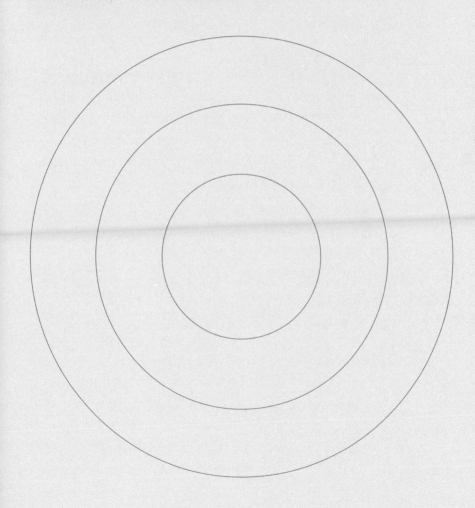

Community and Collaboration

"Community happened when I started to reject the idea that I am what I produce. It happened when I realized that with each success comes a responsibility to examine the infrastructure to which I am contributing."

Sarah Kinlaw

(Composer, choreographer, director, performs as Kinlaw)

There are a number of ways you can support your community. On a fundamental level, you can start by setting intentions around how you want to interact with people. At the beginning of each year, I make a list that serves as a reminder to be a decent human. It usually includes, among other things, be kind, escape ego, and be the person in private you say you are in public.

Another level of community involvement is supporting your friends or colleagues. "Sometimes it's about making a mix that features your friend's music," Drew Daniel explains. "Sometimes it's about proposing a conference panel that brings together grad students and 'stars' in an academic field. You blurb a friend's book to celebrate what they did. In every case, there's a flow in both directions of support and affirmation and advocacy."

George Clarke, singer of the band Deafheaven, describes a network of labor within the arts that is essential but isn't readily seen: "Promoters, space managers, sound technicians, lighting technicians, box-office workers, janitors, bus drivers, rental companies, stagehands; this work is unspoken because it clouds the dreamer's sunset view of what it is to be an artist." Think about getting involved in the creative infrastructure around you by lending your skills to a space or project that you admire.

Take Action

Brainstorm some things that you can do to support your
creative community, or if you prefer, use this space to set
an intention or jot down key words about how you want to be
within your community.

_____

_____

_____

_____

_____

_____

_____

_____

_____

_____

_____

_____

_____

_____

_____

_____

Community Over Algorithms

One day, I tweeted the slogan: "Community over algorithms." What I meant by this was finding a human way to navigate the Internet. We're taught not to read the comments online—and usually I agree—but you can also see this online chorus as a community or potential collaborators. When you post something, do people try to interact with the material? Do they riff on it? A comment that might at first be upsetting can be framed as something constructive. Roxane Gay and Aparna Nancherla both see the possibility of social media as a creative workshop:

"I use [Twitter] as a joke incubator, but I remember going through a period where I felt so immersed in Twitter that I was having trouble writing longer bits. Everything was coming out in these short, little thoughts. If you find you've written fifteen tweets on the same thing, you're like, 'Oh, maybe I can structure all of these around their bigger theme.' In that sense, it's helpful. You're sending out little thoughts and seeing which ones spark."

Aparna Nancherla
(Comedian, actor)*

*Stosuy, Brandon, "Aparna Nancherla on being more than just funny," The Creative Independent, January 4, 2017.

"I often think of Twitter, especially when I'm thinking through current events, like a sandbox. I'm kicking around ideas. There are definitely times when I do latch on to something and think, *this deserves the kind of thought and depth that writing an essay could bring about* . . . When I hit my limit, which I do regularly, I just don't go on Twitter for four days. It's fine. I choose when I want to be part of social media."

Roxane Gay
(Writer, author of *Bad Feminist*, *Hunger*, *Difficult Women*)**

**Stosuy, Brandon, "Roxane Gay on the importance of storytelling," The Creative Independent, November 30, 2016.

Conclusion

Being part of a community means you are *literally part of something*: You collaborate on your own work, you help with other people's projects, and you find inspiration from both.

   To keep the circle of community working, it's important to remember that you don't know everything (nobody is good at *everything*). As Vernon Chatman suggests, collaboration offers a chance to figure out where you shine and where you don't: "If the person you are collaborating with is better and more motivated in one area, it's fun to surrender that zone to them and focus on your own strengths. Your blind trust in a partner can trick them into living up to that trust, and vice versa." It's a good balancing act for the ego.

   We can't idealize ourselves and we shouldn't idealize our community either—utopias don't exist. Clementine and Valentine Nixon, sisters based in rural New Zealand who make music as Purple Pilgrims, describe the complex dynamic that community plays in their creative process: "In our experience, the arts community has been both fruitfully inspiring and stifling. We've experienced both the feeling of a community encouraging us to flourish in whichever direction we please, and its flip side of feeling too comfortable in and restricted by a 'scene' mentality, which eventually pushed us into new experimentation and directions in reaction to the community itself. Both sides of the coin are equally important to our growth."

   I'm involved in multiple scenes, but I also retreat periodically to relative isolation to read more and think. Time alone brings renewed energy and clarity to group projects and collaborations. For many artists, a big part of their practice is about striking a balance between reaching out and retreating. You can make your circle for sharing your work smaller or larger depending on the needs of your process.

The cycle of inspiration we've set up in this book doesn't end with community and finding an audience for your work. You don't arrive at a perfect state, release your work into the world, and call it quits. This is an ongoing process between looking inward and outward for new ideas and ways to move forward with your work and life.

Here are some ways to keep the process going:

> Reflect on why you're making work and whether it's important to you to share it. Putting your art and ideas out there is an exercise in managing ego and vulnerability. Be rooted in your reasons for doing it.

> If you *do* want to share your work, who do you imagine sharing it with first? Decide who you trust and when you want their input.

> Develop an awareness of your strengths and where you need help. Use this self-knowledge to navigate partnerships, creative bartering, and collaborations.

> Create the scene you want to be a part of. Start by choosing a few people that you'd like to bring together to make something. You don't need to be clear on all of the details up front.

> Brainstorm some things you can do to support your creative community, taking note of the unglamorous and necessary things that always need doing.

Acknowledgments

In a book about staying inspired, it makes sense to thank all the people who have inspired you. That would take a separate book, though, so I'll limit myself here.

There are, of course, the folks I reached out to with questions and whose thoughts have made *Stay Inspired* a richer reading experience than if it had just been me talking by myself. Each one inspires me in different ways—through their work, our overlapping projects, and just by being a good person.

I would also like to thank my editor, Karrie Witkin. This is the second book we've done together, but it feels like we've been making books together forever. I'm not being modest when I say *Stay Inspired* would not be nearly as good as it is without her thoughts, insights, and edits. Thanks, too, to my agent, Chad Luibl, who helped me pivot from memoir to how-to to self-help to a combination of all three.

A big thank you, too, to Hayley Salmon for the smart, thoughtful edits (and, who in her first email to me said "just replace the Misfits/punk scene with Blondie and ballet"), and to artist/illustrator/good human Kristian Henson for again making a truly beautiful book.

Every morning I wake up early to write. At some point, one of my sons runs downstairs to tell me about a dream or a fact they remembered about World War II. When I see them, I close my laptop, and I listen. And, throughout the day, I keep listening. Thank you, Henry and Jake, for the daily inspiration.

Thinking about all the projects I did when I was younger, and how they bleed into what I make now, I also wanted to thank my endlessly supportive father, who calls me once a week to see what I'm doing—and he keeps listening, too.

And, it may go without saying, but I'll say it: Thank you to my wife, Jane—it's inspiring how you manage to run your architecture firm, actively participate in community advocacy, help the kids direct their DIY baking and movie projects, and put up with my penchant for now and then singing death metal songs. I couldn't ask for a better life partner (aka life collaborator).